W9-AYP-570

It is July 4, 1836, and Prairietown, Illinois, is celebrating the biggest and most exuberant holiday of the year. This is the "Glorious Fourth," and in Prairietown—and across the country—townfolk and strangers passing through have stopped their day-to-day lives to join together as Americans to commemorate their young nation's birthday.

Patriotism is high, and the festivities are without end. There are parades and speeches; dancing, singing, and playacting; competitions for young and old; a community barbeque with roast pig and the once-a-year special Federal cake—and sparklers all the way from Indianapolis!

Joan Anderson's spirited text and George Ancona's stunning photographs bring to life America's first national holiday. Accurate in every detail, *The Glorious Fourth at Prairietown* was photographed at Conner Prairie Pioneer Settlement, the living-history outdoor museum near Indianapolis, Indiana.

The
Glorious
Fourth
at Prairietown

The Glorious Fourth at Prairietown

by Joan Anderson

photographed by George Ancona

William Morrow and Company, Inc. / New York

To Luke, a spirited pioneer.
J.A.

To Laura, welcome.
G.A.

We would like to thank Polly Jontz and her Conner Prairie staff for making it possible to depict a historically accurate pioneer's Fourth of July.

We are especially grateful to Joe Farah for coordinating all the shots and making impossible setups possible, and for his cordial hospitality. We owe the historical accuracy to David Vanderstel and Dennis Covener's thorough research of Indiana in 1836.

We would like to thank all the interpreters and the interpretation staff, especially Sue Cane who has worked hard on our two latest books, and also Cheryl Roberson and Gregg Jackson. Special feelings and love to P.J. Rutar who played Joshua. Happy Birthday to Sam Dodson and Stephanie Cochran and thank you, too, Myra Church!

And finally, none of the special effects would have been pictured without the coordination of Jim Byers who was able to make anything appear at a moment's notice.

Joan Anderson
George Ancona

Text copyright © 1986 by Joan Anderson   Photographs copyright © 1986 by George Ancona

Printed in the United States of America.   1 2 3 4 5 6 7 8 9 10

Library of Congress Cataloging-in-Publication Data
Anderson, Joan.
The Glorious Fourth at Prairietown.
Summary: Recreates the Fourth of July in 1836 in the fictional village of Prairietown, Indiana, to show how the holiday was celebrated in a typical frontier community.
1. Fourth of July celebrations—Juvenile literature. 2. West (U.S.)—Social life and customs—Juvenile literature. [1. Fourth of July—Indiana. 2. West (U.S.)—Social life and customs] I. Ancona, George, ill. II. Title.
E286.A1243   1986   394.2'684'772   85-28417
ISBN 0-688-06246-6
ISBN 0-688-06247-4 (lib. bdg.)

Joshua Carpenter had been traveling in his family's new Conestoga wagon now for thirty days. He knew for sure how long he, Ma, Pa, and his sister, Becky, had been making their way westward on the National Road because he kept a daily log. The log was the way the family kept track of exactly what day it was and how many miles they had covered.

The date was July 3, 1836. Joshua was thinking back about how it had all happened so sudden—moving, that is. Pa just announced one morning that they were leaving Westmoreland County, Pennsylvania. "Illinois or Iowa," he said. "If we don't go now, those two good tracts of land advertised in *The Journal* will be all bought up." Pa had wanted to relocate for a long time so he could have a real big farm and make extra money from his woodworking business.

Joshua had pleaded with Pa not to leave until after the Fourth of July. Becky and he loved the Fourth, what with all the parades and contests and parties and firecrackers.

"There are only three safe months to travel west," Pa answered. "If we don't leave by June, we'll run into all sorts of problems."

It was sure sad saying good-bye to Grandpa and Grandma. Joshua was brave, but his eyes had filled up with tears when he waved good-bye. As for his best friend, Ethan, well, that was one of the good parts of keeping the log. Once they settled, he planned to write Ethan every detail about their trip.

The trip was lonely. They were traveling by themselves and usually didn't see another wagon for days. Sometimes they'd camp with a family they happened upon. Joshua was happy when they did, since he'd heard tell that folks had been known to go crazy on long wagon trips.

Becky was scared out of her wits half the time by the tales she'd heard about Indians, but Joshua didn't have much time to get frightened. There were so many chores to do. Sometimes he even rode up on Henry's back and drove the wagon. Once in a while, he'd find time to snuggle into his tick under the canvas cover away from the hot sun and read the dictionary or play on his penny whistle.

Pa figured that if a wheel didn't bust or the rivers weren't flooded, they might get near Indianapolis for the Fourth. So today, Joshua sat high up on the wagon seat squished between Ma and Pa, hoping to spot something on the horizon. His arithmetic told him that they should be nearing a city, but his eyes told him they were still miles from anywhere.

"Oh, well," Joshua thought. "If we don't get to Indianapolis by tomorrow, it probably doesn't really matter. After all, how could the Fourth on the prairie compare to Pennsylvania? Why, Pennsylvania was the very place where the Declaration of Independence was signed, and so many important Americans lived there . . . Benjamin Franklin, Betsy Ross, William Penn."

The horses clomped along as the wagon jiggled and creaked. Their belongings rattled as they went over bump after bump. Joshua could hardly concentrate under such conditions. Besides, he felt anxious. So he grabbed his penny whistle and started to play "Yankee Doodle." Before he knew it, the whole family was singing.

Even Jack and Henry seemed spurred on by the song. The horses were trotting along faster than ever. The family continued singing until, suddenly, off in the distance, Joshua noticed something. He stopped playing, stood up to see better, then shouted.

"Pa, out there, *look!*"

"Where?" Pa asked, squinting off in the direction of his son's finger.

"Doesn't that look like a town to you?"

"Yep, it sure does," Pa agreed, pulling on the reins to slow down the horses.

"Could we head on over?" Joshua asked. "It might be small, but it sure looks good."

"I don't see why not," Pa said, yelling giddap.

Everyone was silent, except Becky. She had begun counting, "One, two, three, four, five, six . . ."

"You pick the strangest times to do your learning," Joshua teased his sister, who had been practicing her numbers and letters the whole trip.

"I'm not practicing numbers," she answered angrily. "I'm counting buildings. So far as I can see, this place is about the biggest we've passed since Springfield, Ohio."

She was right, Joshua thought. At least from far away, it looked pretty fine.

The Carpenters made their way onto a
street. Pa said halt when he saw a man with a
friendly-looking face. "Good day," he said.
"We're the Carpenters from Pennsylvania. My
son here figures we must be in Indiana."

"Your son's a smart youngin'. This here is
Prairietown, Indiana. My name's Ben Curtis."

"Pleased to meet ya," Pa said, tipping his hat. "We were wondering if there'd be a spot we could camp outside the village?"

"Sure is," Mr. Curtis replied, "and we'd be pleased to have ya. We're expecting plenty of strangers and neighbors, what with the Fourth being tomorrow." Joshua and Becky grinned at each other when they heard this. "Go on over there," Mr. Curtis continued, "and turn off at the bend in the road. You'll find a good place for camping behind Doc Campbell's barn; plenty of feed for the horses, too."

"Mighty grateful," Pa answered.

No sooner had they tied up the horses than a townswoman introduced herself. "I know you must be tired and dusty," she said, "and anxious to get supper on." Ma nodded yes with a sigh. "Mr. McClure's got a good pump behind his house," she said, pointing to a neat little white building. "Your youngster can get all the water you need."

"Why, thank you," Ma said.

"And as for your daughter here, you just come with me. I'll give you a load of firewood and some fresh biscuits. I just put them up today for the festivities tomorrow."

"How nice of you," Ma said gratefully. "We surely haven't had the likes of biscuits for weeks."

Joshua headed to the McClures'. By the time he brought the bucket of water back, Ma didn't look so weary. The soup was beginning to smell awfully tasty, and his belly told him it was ready for supper. Just then there was a loud bang.

"Indians!" Becky yelled.

"Not in civilization, silly," Joshua answered. *Bang. Bang. Bang. Bang.* "Those aren't no guns. That's firecrackers!" Turning to his pa, Joshua asked if he could go exploring.

"I suppose there's no harm," Pa answered, "just so you're back before sunset."

Joshua ran off, letting his ears direct him to the very end of the street.

Peering out from behind a big tree, he saw two boys lighting the fanciest crackers he had ever seen.

"Well, good day there, Pennsylvania boy," a voice from nowhere said. Joshua turned and saw Mr. Curtis, the friendly man who had greeted them earlier. "C'mon over and meet my boys, Thomas and Edward."

Joshua stuck out his hand.

"Want to light one?" Thomas Curtis asked.

"Can I?" Joshua responded. He was amazed at how much Thomas looked like his best friend, Ethan.

"Sure," he answered, handing Joshua one.

Edward ran into his pa's blacksmith shop and returned with hot coals. He held them to the wick and told Joshua not to let go. "They're pretty, that's all. They don't explode."

"Where'd you get them? I've never seen ones like this."

"Pa brought 'em back from Indianapolis. We have more!" Edward announced eagerly.

"Well, I sure would like to have some," Joshua said. "Could we maybe trade?"

Thomas looked at Edward. "Well, they *are* mighty dear," he said slowly, "but I reckon maybe."

Joshua thought fast about what he'd brought with him. "I've got some machine-made things," he suggested.

That seemed to please the Curtis boys. "We'll show you around on the way back to your wagon," they suggested.

There was activity everywhere.

"That's Patience Higby dressing up the general store," Thomas pointed out. "The noon ceremony will be there."

"Yeah, and we're having a parade and barbecue, too!" Edward announced excitedly.

"There's Silas McClure. Don't know why he's building a fence today except his grouchy pa probably wants to keep the strangers off his property. Maggie and Suzannah Fenton live over there," Thomas continued. "They're friends of our sister's."

As they rounded the bend, there was noise coming from the Golden Eagle Inn. "Must be them actors Mrs. Campbell hired to perform tomorrow," Thomas commented. Sure enough, a rehearsal was in progress.

"You mean there's going to be a play?" Joshua asked. He'd never seen a real drama before.

"Yep," they answered casually. "Some folks don't take to Mrs. Campbell's culture, but we think it's fun. These special doin's bring our school friends to town. Jonas Foster and Horatio Hawkins will be here for sure."

Joshua couldn't believe he'd come to a spot with so many youngin's to do things with. After living in a wagon for a month, this sure was a treat. But with all that was going on, he had lost track of time. Suddenly he realized that the sun was practically set and Ma would be expecting him to lug the iron kettle off to be washed. This wasn't the time for a trade.

"I've got to be getting back for chores before my pa gets angry. Do you suppose we could trade first thing in the morning, instead of right now?" Joshua cautiously asked his new friends.

"Sure thing," Thomas answered. "Sounds like your pa's the same as ours."

Joshua was relieved as they split up at the end of the road after agreeing to meet the next morning at the general store.

Joshua gobbled down his soup, and by the time he cleaned the kettle, he was ready for bed. What a day! He pulled his tick out, tucked it snugly under the wagon, and let the cool prairie breezes lull him to sleep.

The next thing he knew, someone was whistling his favorite Fourth of July song, "Hail, Columbia." Was he dreaming, or was the big day here?

He opened his eyes to find everyone awake and dressed but him! Tossing his tick into the wagon and rummaging through his sack, he grabbed the first few tradables he could find. Becky watched and figured he was up to something.

"I'm trading for fireworks," he whispered. "If you don't let on to Ma and Pa, I'll get some for you."

Becky loved the sound of fireworks, just as she took to most things boys liked.

"Want to come with me?" Joshua asked her. "The Curtis boys have a sister, and lots of other girls are coming to town today."

Becky needed no more convincing.

They spotted the Curtis brothers on the benches in front of the general store. When Joshua pulled out his trade, Becky waited under the big maple tree. Not only did the boys willingly exchange the jacks and marbles for two packets of loud crackers, but they also gave Joshua some rock candy. Joshua took a bite and saved the rest for Becky, who liked candy better than anyone else in the family.

Suddenly there came the sound of a drum roll. "The muster," Edward shouted. "Hurry, we can't miss the parade!"

Everyone headed for the Golden Eagle Inn, which was crowded with spectactors. Standing in front of it, yelling at the top of his lungs, was Colonel G. Benjamin Johnson, head of the Prairietown Militia. He was trying to organize his motley-looking troops.

"Fall in!" he shouted. "And that don't mean into the tavern. We'll never get this procession going if any of you hit the Golden Eagle. This is a good and serious day. So be dignified."

"This militia looks awful different," Joshua said to Thomas. "Back home, ours have matching uniforms and are like real army men."

"Well, here they don't mean much . . . I mean as far as protection," Thomas answered. "Pa says that the militia get together once a month for rifle practice 'cause the Constitution says all men must be able to use a gun."

"Forward, move," the Colonel ordered. "Hep, two, three, four." The procession was under way. "Count cadence," he shouted when he noticed most of the men were out of step.

That didn't matter to Joshua. He thought it looked real pretty with the flag blowing almost to the rhythm of the fife music and some ladies waving their handkerchiefs.

The militia stopped once by Doc Campbell's to escort Mr. Samuel Hastings, the town war hero, to the noon ceremony.

Joshua and Becky joined their parents once the parade reached the general store. A handsome-looking man who had been sitting on the porch rose and stood behind a barrel. "For those of you who are visiting today," he announced, "my name is Mr. Solomon Hudson. I am the justice of the peace of Prairietown and most honored to welcome you all to our nation's sixtieth birthday."

Everyone cheered. Joshua loved it.

"It has been a mere sixty years since we declared our freedom from the oppressive rule of Great Britain. Let us think today of our beloved first president, George Washington, as well as of Thomas Jefferson and John Adams, who just ten years ago today departed from this world. We have survived so much . . . our young nation was victorious in two great wars, the Revolution and the War of 1812. Not long ago, our own Mr. Hastings, sitting here beside me, fought in the battle of Tippecanoe, right here in Indiana."

There were more cheers. Everyone was full of such spirit, Joshua thought.

"Today we welcome travelers from as far away as Pennsylvania . . ."

"That's us he's talking about," Joshua whispered to Becky.

". . . and others from neighboring farms and villages. But we are not strangers. No, we are part of the huge American family.

"So now, in keeping with the spirit of our country's natal day, let us join with the Prairietown Singers in the singing of "Ode for the Fourth of July.""

It sounded like "My Country 'Tis of Thee," Joshua thought, and he began to sing loud and strong. Even though his words were different from those being sung, it didn't matter. He felt proud to be an American. He realized as he sang that, no matter where he was from, today especially he was not a boy from Pennsylvania, he was simply an American boy.

"And now the most special moment of all," Mr. Hudson continued, "the reading of the Declaration of Independence."

A brief cheer went up from the crowd, and then there was silence. Joshua intended to listen real hard to every word. Now that he was almost a grown-up, he figured he ought to understand such an important document.

"When in the course of human events, it becomes necessary for one people to dissolve the political bands which have connected them with another . . ."

Joshua was lost in the rhetoric, but shouts of "Long live the Republic" jolted him out of his thoughts. Some people were yelling, "To the United States of America," and others cried, "To Indiana, the Hoosier State."

The sound of fiddle music now filled the air, and off the porch stepped a man playing a lively tune.

"Grab your partners, two by two," he shouted to the rhythm, "and chassé down to form a line." Within seconds, the solemnity of the moment broke into joyous celebration. Men took their ladies gently under the arm, while others stood nearby clapping and tapping their toes.

Joshua and his pa moved over to a nearby fence to be out of the way of the swirling dancers. "Well, son, I reckon this is going to be a mighty fine day."

"It already is, Pa," Joshua answered. "I tried real hard to listen to the Declaration. I mean, it sounds real good and important, but I still don't quite understand what it means."

"Well, Joshua, I reckon the best way to explain it to you is to think about it in terms of our family. This here Declaration is the commemoration of our freedom and independence. That's something our family is exercising right now. We're moving west and didn't have to ask permission from any authority to go. We can live as we please and do just about anything we want within the law. Does that explain it any better?"

"Yes, Pa, I suppose it does."

They were interrupted by the sounds of a commotion coming from across the courtyard. "Mrs. Carson's serving her stack cake," Edward Curtis yelled to everyone. "She only makes it for us on the Fourth of July, so come and get it."

Joshua was hungry. He ran over, grabbing a piece of cake just like everyone else, and garbled a thank-you as the applesauce filling melted in his mouth.

"Let's head up to the dramatic show," someone suggested, and off the children went.

They got sidetracked when they saw Mr. Tripplett, the itinerant phrenologist, reading the bumps on old Mr. McClure's head.

"What's phrenology?" Joshua asked in a loud voice as he read a nearby sign.

Before anyone could answer, Mr. Tripplett suggested that Joshua step right up and see.

"How old are you, young feller?" Mr. Tripplett asked while moving his hands around Joshua's skull.

"Almost twelve, sir," the boy answered.

Mr. Tripplett's hands stopped. "Aha, I feel here that you have the faculty of benevolence. You want to do good, but sometimes it's hard. That true?"

"I suppose so," Joshua answered. "I wish I could behave better, especially in school."

"Uh-huh, and right back here, another bump tells me you seek approbativeness."

"Huh?" Joshua asked.

Mr. Tripplett explained that Joshua liked a lot of approval.

"Oh, yes," he admitted, "I especially like it when I please my pa, but it's mighty hard to act like a grown-up all the time."

"Well," Mr. Tripplett said, "you're gettin' to the age when it comes natural. I feel here you have the gift of tongue. That'll be a help, son."

Joshua was getting itchy sitting so long with everyone staring. "I learned a lot, sir," he said, getting up quickly before Mr. Tripplett found more bumps.

He hurried back to his friends and said, "It sure is hot. Anyplace we could take a swim?"

"The water hole," Thomas Curtis yelled, and they all hightailed it to the pond, unbuttoning their shirts and trousers along the way. Joshua was the first to dive in. After a quick swim, the water fights began, which turned out to be a big mistake. The noise they made trailed up the hill right to the spot where the girls had begun a game of quoits. Becky Carpenter couldn't resist playing a joke on her brother. At her suggestion, the girls crept quietly through the woods, collected almost all the clothes, and ran off quickly before the boys even noticed.

"Come back here," the boys yelled. "You can't do this."

"Oh, no?" the girls teased from the woods.

"Well," said Thomas, "we've got no choice. Someone's got to get our pants back." Jonas Foster knew he'd be the one. He was the youngest and always had to do the dirty work.

Swimming to the pond's edge, he reached for the nearest shirt, wrapped it around himself, and ran in search of the clothes. He found them piled on a log and carried everything back to a triumphant cheer.

As soon as the boys dressed, they had only one intention—to find the girls. They came upon them knee-deep in a game of hoops. Ma and Pa were there, cheering on Becky. Joshua joined in, even though he was still a little angry. Being on a wagon trail with Becky for so long, he'd come to realize that his sister was now just about his best friend.

"C'mon, Becky," he hooted. "Keep it going. You can do it!"

Thomas Curtis meanwhile announced to the others that this sure wasn't the time to get back at the girls. "We might just as well head down to Shooters Hollow and catch the end of the rifle contest," he suggested.

Joshua was torn. He wanted to see if Becky would win. He knew she could; but he also knew the day was almost over and being with friends was important, too. So off he went, and got there just in time to see Asa Taylor eliminated from the competition. The contest was down to just two men—Caleb Bartholomew and Lieutenant Amick.

Joshua could tell from the shouts that most of the spectators were for Caleb. He stood behind the supply table, where he had a perfect view.

Colonel Johnson, who was running the contest, gave the final rules. "The best of five shots will be the winner. Are ya ready?" The two men nodded. "All right, then, Mr. Bartholomew, you draw first."

Caleb packed just enough powder so he wouldn't get a kickback. He held his rifle mighty steady, took aim, and fired.

"Looks good from here," old Mr. Whitaker, the judge, proclaimed after looking through his telescope.

Next, it was Lieutenant Amick's turn. After his shot, they alternated shots until each had his five. Joshua could see the tension in Caleb's face as the Colonel and Mr. Whitaker walked down into the hollow to inspect the targets. When they returned, they paused. The crowd became quiet.

"And the winner is . . . " Mr. Whitaker said, dragging out the suspense as long as he could, "Caleb Bartholomew! Go pick out any hog ya want, son," he said, patting Caleb on the back while the crowd cheered.

Some followed Caleb over to watch which hog he'd pick, while the aroma from the barbecue pit made others simply take their bodies in that direction.

"Gosh, I am hungry," Joshua thought. Aside from some cake, candy, and lemonade, he hadn't seen much eating all day. Some folks brought baskets of food to town, but, it being the Fourth, most womenfolk were celebrating by not cooking.

No sooner had the thought of eating crossed Joshua's mind than a banging pot announced that the pig was plum ready.

"Git over here, Samuel Cox and David Fenton," Miss Patience Higby ordered. "Ada Noreen and I have been slavin' over this here animal all day. Time you fellers took it off the spit and did the carvin.'"

As Joshua moved over closer to the table, he saw a group of men gathered around. Pa was in the midst of them, raising a cup and about to make a toast.

"To this fine and friendly country of ours, and most especially to the folks of Prairietown. The Carpenter family is most grateful for your hospitality," he said.

"Hear, hear," the men added, as Joshua watched Pa with pride.

Just then the roasted pig was placed on the table.

"Sure smells delicious," Becky said, coming over to Joshua.

Many folks had gathered around by now to help serve. "You done a fine job, Miss Higby," someone said. "That there hog is ready to be ate."

The men and women began to hack away, grabbing pieces as they came off the knives. Joshua filled his plate, having not tasted meat for an awful long time.

Just as he was about to get in line for a second helping, Mrs. McClure stepped forth with her federal cake.

"Hmm, it's good," Becky said to her friends after taking a lick. "But why's it so special?"

"Well, we use seven whole eggs, lots of white sugar, and finely ground flour, that's why," Mary McClure declared. "Ma only makes it on the Fourth."

The day was coming to an end. Folks continued eating till the table was bare. Some ladies relaxed in the shade while their men continued a lengthy political debate. Edward Curtis was being dragged off for evening chores. As for Joshua, he watched nostalgically until the last visitor took leave.

Very early the next morning, the Carpenter family headed out of Prairietown. Joshua wished he could stay on another day or so, or forever. But he knew better. A big chunk of land near Prairietown would cost more than Pa could afford.

Nevertheless, he had learned so much during their visit here. He used to think that Westmoreland County, Pennsylvania, was the only special place in America. Now he knew that there were other places, like Prairietown, where life was good and folks were just as special. He felt sad to have to say good-bye to new friends, yet he felt hopeful that Illinois or Iowa would have people just as good as here. As he waved good-bye, he drank in the view, hoping to never forget the Glorious Fourth of 1836.

Afterword

In 1836 the United States was only sixty years old, patriotism was high, and, regardless of where in the existing twenty-five states one hailed from, Americans reached out to one another as they had done from the very first Fourth of July, in 1776, to celebrate their one commonality—the birth of their nation.

Anything that breathed the spirit of national patriotism was important to these new Americans, many of whom remembered both the Revolutionary War and the War of 1812. And, because they needed a tie that would bind them together, this "Jubilee in July" was celebrated with much enthusiasm across the land.

At this time, Fourth of July was the nation's *only* holiday—Thanksgiving, Christmas, Memorial and Veteran's Days all rolled into one. Thanksgiving did not become a national holiday until after the Civil War, and Christmas was celebrated in a simple fashion according to an individual family's religious and ethnic customs. Therefore, anticipation for the Fourth was high, especially among the children—very much like it is today before Christmas. This was not because gifts were exchanged, but because the Fourth was the only day of the year when youngsters were free from school and chores.

People everywhere paraded through the streets, gathered at noontime to read the Declaration of Independence and to make flowery speeches about America's forefathers—and together celebrated their "sweet land of liberty."

—*Joan Anderson*